DEAR ELIZABETH

Sarah Ruhl's plays include *In the Next Room, or the vibrator play* (Pulitzer Prize finalist; Tony Award nominee for best new play); *The Clean House* (Pulitzer Prize finalist, 2005; winner of the Susan Smith Blackburn Prize); *Passion Play: a cycle* (PEN American Award); *Dead Man's Cell Phone* (Helen Hayes Award); and, most recently, *Stage Kiss* and *Dear Elizabeth*.

Her many plays have been produced on Broadway, off-Broadway, regionally throughout the country, and internationally. They have been translated into more than fifteen languages, including Polish, Russian, Korean, and Arabic.

Originally from Chicago, Ruhl received her M.F.A. from Brown University, where she studied with Paula Vogel. Ruhl has since been the recipient of a MacArthur Fellowship, the Helen Merrill Emerging Playwright Award, the Whiting Writers' Award, the PEN/Laura Pels International Foundation for Theater Award for a mid-career playwright, a Feminist Press's Forty Under Forty Award, and the 2010 Lilly Award. She is currently on the faculty of the Yale School of Drama and lives in Brooklyn with her family.

ALSO BY SARAH RUHL

DEAR ELIZABETH

DEAR ELIZABETH

A Play in Letters
from Elizabeth Bishop to Robert Lowell
and Back Again

SARAH RUHL

Farrar, Straus and Giroux
New York

Farrar, Straus and Giroux
18 West 18th Street, New York 10011

Library of Congress Cataloging-in-Publication Data
Ruhl, Sarah, 1974–
    Dear Elizabeth : a play in letters from Elizabeth Bishop to Robert
Lowell and back again / Sarah Ruhl. — First edition.
        pages   cm
        ISBN 978-0-86547-815-2 (paperback) — ISBN 978-0-374-71198-6
(ebook)
        1. Bishop, Elizabeth, 1911–1979—Correspondence—Drama.
    2. Lowell, Robert, 1917–1977—Correspondence—Drama.   3. Poets,
American—20th century—Biography—Drama.   I. Title.

PS3618.U48 D43 2014
812'.6—dc23

                                                                    2014004042

Our books may be purchased in bulk for promotional, educational, or
business use. Please contact your local bookseller or the Macmillan Corporate and
Premium Sales Department at 1-800-221-7945, extension 5442, or by e-mail at
MacmillanSpecialMarkets@macmillan.com.

www.fsgbooks.com
www.twitter.com/fsgbooks • www.facebook.com/fsgbooks

3 5 7 9 10 8 6 4

For Elizabeth B and Elizabeth C as in Charuvastra who covered her typewriter with bandages and typed out all the poetry she could remember when she was far from home

Sometimes it seems . . . as though only intelligent people are stupid enough to fall in love & only stupid people are intelligent enough to let themselves be loved.

—Elizabeth Bishop, from her notebook

Dream—

I see a postman everywhere
Vanishing in thin blue air,
A mammoth letter in his hand,
Postmarked from a foreign land.

The postman's uniform is blue.
The letter is of course from you
And I'd be able to read, I hope,
My own name on the envelope

But he has trouble with this letter
Which constantly grows bigger & bigger
And over and over with a stare,
He vanishes in blue, blue air.

—Elizabeth Bishop, *Edgar Allan Poe & The Juke-Box:*
Uncollected Poems, Drafts, and Fragments

Elizabeth told me about Robert Lowell. She said, "He's my best friend." When I met him a few years later, I mentioned that I knew her and he said, "Oh, she's my best friend." It was nice to think that she and Lowell both thought of each other in the same way.

—Thom Gunn, *Remembering Elizabeth Bishop*

I can remember Cal's carrying Elizabeth's "Armadillo" poem around in his wallet everywhere, not the way you'd carry the picture of a grandson, but as you'd carry something to brace you and make you sure of how a poem ought to be.

—Richard Wilbur, *Remembering Elizabeth Bishop*

While we were with her, she managed to finish "North Haven," the poem [or elegy] for Lowell. She read it to us and walked about with it in her hand. I found it very moving that she felt she could hardly bear to put it down, that it was part of her. She put it beside her plate at dinner.

—Ilse Barker, *Remembering Elizabeth Bishop*

Contents

Preface

The great poets Elizabeth Bishop and Robert Lowell were great friends, and they wrote more than eight hundred pages of letters to each other. When I was on bed rest, pregnant with twins, a friend gave me the book of their collected letters, *Words in Air: The Complete Correspondence Between Elizabeth Bishop and Robert Lowell.* I already had a long-standing obsession with Bishop; my obsession with Lowell and his friendship with Bishop now began. I could not put the letters down. I hungered to hear them read aloud; I particularly longed to hear letter number 161 read out loud. Number 161 is Lowell's most confessional letter to Bishop, and I think, one of the most beautiful love letters ever written. In it, he says, about *not* asking Bishop to marry him: "But asking you is *the* might have been for me, the one towering change, the other life that might have been had."

Reading these eight hundred pages—these strands of two lives intersecting, rarely meeting—I thought: Why do I find this narrative so compelling, even though theirs is not a story in the traditional sense? I was desperate to know how the "story" would come out—how each life would progress, how the relationship would end. But I also loved how the letters resisted a sense of the usual literary "story"—how instead they forced us to look at life as it is lived. Not neat. Not two glorious Greek arcs meeting in the center. Instead: a dialectic between the interior poetic life and the pear-shaped, particular, sudden, ordinary life-as-it-is-lived.

Life intrudes, without warning. Bishop's great love and partner, Lota, commits suicide without warning. Bishop has multiple asthma attacks, and often needs to be hospitalized for alcoholism and depression. Lowell dies suddenly of a heart attack in a taxicab en route to see his ex-wife Elizabeth Hardwick. As he died in the taxi he held a painting of his third wife, painted by her ex-husband, Lucian Freud. Lowell had bipolar disorder and often found himself quite suddenly in a sanatorium. Bishop and Lowell's carefully built, Platonic poetic worlds are intruded on constantly by the vagaries of life and the body. And through such sudden disturbances, their letters were like lanterns sent to each other across long distances. Bishop lived in Brazil most of her life, and Lowell lived in New York, Boston, and London. Their friendship was lived largely on paper, though they met up at crucial times in their lives.

Bishop was in New York when Lota committed suicide, and she stayed at Hardwick and Lowell's apartment. They paid for her ambulance ride through Central Park, the result of a bad fall she took, perhaps induced by too much drink, after Lota's suicide. Bishop was plagued her whole life by alcoholism; at one point a friend eliminated all the liquor in her house and Bishop was reduced to drinking rubbing alcohol and ended up in the hospital. Lowell visited Bishop in South America and was hospitalized in Argentina for a manic episode.

Their correspondence spans political epochs—coups in Brazil, the Vietnam War—personal epochs, and literary epochs. Bishop observes Lowell's trajectory as he creates the confessional movement in poetry. There is, in the letters, an extraordinary dialectic between Lowell's more confessional mode and Bishop's formal restraint. Her skeptical attitude toward the confessional, however, didn't keep her from loving Lowell's poetry. They both carried each other's poems in their minds and in their pockets. Lowell carried Bishop's "The Armadillo" (a poem she dedicated to Lowell) in his wallet, a kind of talisman. Lowell wrote "Skunk Hour" for Bishop, as well as many sonnets and a poem called "Water," about a seminal weekend the two of them spent in Maine.

After Lowell divorced Jean Stafford in July 1948, he visited Bishop in Maine. It's a visit they would both return to again and again in their letters and in their poetry. It's impossible to reconstruct exactly what happened; we know from letters and poems that they spent the weekend together, at one point standing waist high in water, and Bishop said to Lowell, "When you write my epitaph, you must say I was the loneliest person who ever lived." Bishop wrote later that they were: "Swimming, or rather standing, numb to the waist in the freezing cold water, but continuing to talk. If I were to think of any Saint in his connection then it is St. Sebastian—he stood in a rocky basin of the freezing water sloshing it over his handsome youthful body and I could almost see the arrows sticking out of him."

We know that shortly after that visit, Lowell told some

friends he was going to marry Bishop. Soon after, they had a drunken weekend at Bard where many poets were gathered. Lowell was rumored to have proposed to Bishop that weekend. Bishop wrote to another friend, "Saturday night was worst—a really drunken party, I'm afraid, with everyone behaving very much the way poets are supposed to." In another account, Bishop remembers that she and Hardwick had helped a drunken Lowell back to his room, taken off his shoes and tie, loosened his shirt, upon which Hardwick said, "Why, he's an Adonis!" and Bishop said, "from then on I knew it was all over."

We also know from their friend Joseph Summers that at the end of the Bard weekend, "He and Elizabeth seemed to be very much in love . . . He was saying, 'Now let me know when you are coming back.' And she said, 'I don't know.' 'Let me know where you are,' and so on." Another friend reports, "She told us at one point she loved Cal more than anybody she'd ever known, except for Lota, but that he would destroy her." And from another friend: Lowell "was one of the few people Bishop addressed in her poems. She said that he had proposed to her, and she had turned him down." Apparently her greatest regret was not having a child, and she considered having one with Lowell early on, but worried about the history of mental illness in both of their families.

The gaps between their letters, the mysterious interludes in which Lowell and Bishop actually saw each other, leaves much to the imagination. Their letters are so hyper-articulate that one almost has the impression that no bits of life were lived without having been written down. These silences between the letters fascinated me as much as the letters themselves. But rather than invent dialogue for these interludes in which they actually met, I felt it important to let Bishop and Lowell speak only in their own words. Bishop's reserve, and her insistence on not mixing fact and fiction, was always with me as I arranged the letters. All the words from the play are taken from their letters and from their poetry.

There are many ways to do this play. One can imagine the full spectacle I have suggested in the stage directions, complete with planets appearing and water rushing onto the stage, as in its premiere at Yale Repertory Theatre. I wanted to see the images in their letters made three-dimensional, to somehow see the reach of their imagery. But I'm also interested in how much the language can do all by itself. One can imagine, for example, a simple book-club version. I saw pictures of one such event in Illinois and was very moved by the simplicity of nonactors who loved poetry reading the letters out loud to fellow travelers. One could also imagine doing the play in a library, at a poetry foundation, or even on the set for another play on a dark Monday night. You really need nothing more than a table and two chairs for two wonderful actors who could even read the letters straight from the page rather than memorizing them. A third actor could read stage directions in place of the projected subtitles.

Regardless of how the play is performed, in a theater or in a room, when I first read the letters, I felt that they demanded to be read out loud, whether by actors or by laypeople. Bishop and Lowell had unerring, consummate ears, and they wrote poetry for a time when Lowell could command massive crowds in Madison Square Garden, all gathered to hear him read his poems. I offer this arrangement, then, in the spirit of a contemporary hunger to hear poetry out loud. I think we are starved for the sound of poetry. I wonder if Bishop and Lowell are among the last great people of letters to write out their lives in letter form. Their letters become almost a medieval church constructed in praise of friendship. It's difficult to write about friendship. Our culture is inundated with stories of romantic love. We understand how romantic love begins, how it ends. We don't understand, in neat narrative fashion, how friendship begins, how it endures. And yet life would be unbearable without friendship.

—Sarah Ruhl

DEAR ELIZABETH

Dear Elizabeth was first commissioned by and produced at the Yale Repertory Theatre (James Bundy, artistic director; Victoria Nolan, managing director; Jennifer Kiger, associate artistic director). The first performance was on November 30, 2012.

Cast

ELIZABETH BISHOP   Mary Beth Fisher
ROBERT LOWELL   Jefferson Mays

Creative Team

DIRECTOR   Les Waters
SCENIC DESIGNER   Adam Rigg
COSTUME DESIGNER   Maria Hooper
LIGHTING DESIGNER   Russell H. Champa
SOUND DESIGNER   Bray Poor
PROJECTION DESIGNER   Hannah Wasileski
PRODUCTION DRAMATURG   Amy Boratko
CASTING   Tara Rubin
STAGE MANAGER   Kirstin Hodges

Subsequently produced by the Berkeley Repertory Theatre (Tony Taccone, artistic director; Susan Medak, managing director; Liesl Tommy, associate director; Karen Racanelli, general manager). The first performance was on May 24, 2013, at the Roda Theatre.

Cast

ELIZABETH BISHOP Mary Beth Fisher
ROBERT LOWELL Tom Nelis

Creative Team

DIRECTOR Les Waters
SCENIC DESIGNER Annie Smart
COSTUME DESIGNER Maria Hooper
LIGHTING DESIGNER Russell H. Champa
SOUND DESIGNER Bray Poor
PROJECTION DESIGNER Hannah Wasileski
STAGE MANAGER Cynthia Cahill

Subsequently produced by People's Light & Theatre Company (Abigail Adams, artistic director; Ellen Anderson, general manager; Zak Berkman, producing director). The first performance was on April 2, 2014.

Cast

ELIZABETH BISHOP   Ellen McLaughlin
ROBERT LOWELL   Rinde Eckert

Creative Team

DIRECTOR   Lisa Rothe
SCENIC DESIGNER   Jason Simms
COSTUME DESIGNER   Theresa Squire
LIGHTING DESIGNER   Mary Louise Geiger
COMPOSER / SOUND DESIGNER   Rinde Eckert
ASSOCIATE SOUND DESIGNER   Elizabeth Atkinson
PRODUCTION STAGE MANAGER   Kelly O'Rourke
DRAMATURGS   Zak Berkman and Gina Pisasale
LINE PRODUCER   Zak Berkman

Personages
Elizabeth Bishop: a woman between the ages of forty and sixty.
Robert Lowell: a man between the ages of forty and sixty.

Set
One might use subtitles to indicate the place and date of some letters.
A spare set, with two chairs and a table.
One record player, one microphone.
The possibility of the stage becoming, for a moment, the sea and a giant rock, and then back to two private spaces for two writers.
Stagehands might be used to deliver props and glasses of wine to the actors.

Note
The following words are all Elizabeth Bishop's and Robert Lowell's. On occasion I repeated a phrase that they once used, and I often cut internally within their letters. A careful reader

can go back to the original letters (*Words in Air: The Complete Correspondence Between Elizabeth Bishop and Robert Lowell*) to see the letters in their entirety. The numbering of the letters in the afterword corresponds with the numbers in *Words in Air.*

I don't believe the actors should ever pretend to actually *write* the letters. They are speaking the letters to each other and to the audience as though they are in the act of composing them. They should feel in the moment of discovering the thought for the first time.

They might even read them from the page at times. My first impulse when creating this piece was mainly to hear these letters read out loud. So I can imagine full productions of the play, including water, ladders, and moons; and I can also imagine stripped-down versions in which the main event is hearing two actors, or two readers, simply read the thing out loud in a room.

ACT ONE

Part One: Water

Elizabeth Bishop and Robert Lowell enter and sit at a table.

A SUBTITLE FLASHES: May 12, 1947.

BISHOP
Dear Mr. Lowell,

I just wanted to say that I think it is wonderful you have received all the awards; the Guggenheim, the Pulitzer, and—I guess I'll just call them 1, 2, & 3 . . .

Maybe if you're still in town you would come to see me sometime, I should like to see you very much, or just write me a note if you'd rather . . .

Elizabeth Bishop

LOWELL
Dear Miss Bishop,

Sorry to have missed dining with you yesterday, and reading with you. You are a marvelous writer, and your note was about the only one that meant anything to me.

Last night at three we had a fire. The man who started it fell asleep drunk and smoking. He ran back and forth from his room to the bathroom carrying a waste-basket with a thimble-full of water shouting at the top of his lungs, "Shush, shush, no fire. Stop shouting you'll wake everyone up. An accident. Nobody injured," until a policeman shouted: "Nobody injured? Look at all the people you've gotten up." Today my room smells like burnt tar-paper.

I'm going to Boston on the 2nd and then to Yaddo. I hope that I will see more of you some day.

Robert Lowell

BISHOP

Dear Robert,

(I've never been able to catch that name they call you but Mr. Lowell doesn't sound right, either.) I had meant to write to you quite a while ago, to answer the note you sent me in New York, and I certainly meant to do it before your review of my book appeared, but it's too late now.

It is the first review I've had that attempted to find any general drift or consistency in the individual poems and I was beginning to feel there probably wasn't any at all . . . I suppose for pride's sake I should take some sort of stand about the adverse criticisms, but I agreed with some of them only too well—you spoke out my worst fears as well as some of my ambitions . . .

Elizabeth Bishop turns away from the audience for a moment.
Robert Lowell looks up, looking for her.
The vague sound of wind and an indeterminate cow sound.

Robert Lowell looks confused.
Elizabeth Bishop turns back toward the audience.

Heavens—it is an hour later—I was called out to see a calf being born in the pasture beside the house. In five minutes after several falls on its nose it was standing up shaking its head and trying to nurse. They took it away from its mother almost immediately. It seems that if they take the calf away immediately then they don't have the trouble of weaning it—it will drink out of a dish.

The calf's mother has started to moo, and the cow in the next pasture is mooing even louder, possibly in sympathy.

I hope you're liking Yaddo—I almost went there once but changed my mind.

Sincerely yours,
Elizabeth Bishop

LOWELL
Dear Elizabeth:

(You must be called that; I'm called Cal, but I won't explain why. None of the prototypes are flattering: Calvin, Caligula, Caliban, Calvin Coolidge . . .)

I'm glad you wrote me, because it gives me an excuse to tell you how much I liked your *New Yorker* fish poem. Perhaps, it's your best. Anyway, I felt very envious reading it.

I question a little the word *breast* in the last four or five lines—a little too much in its context perhaps; but I'm probably wrong.

She thinks he is wrong.

P.S. I'd like to have you record your poems when you come here. I hope you'll really come here this fall and we can go to the galleries and see the otters.

Yours,

Cal

BISHOP

Dear Cal,

I think I'd rather see the otters than make recordings, but I am quite sure I'll be there for a day or two, and I'd like to see you, recordings or no.

P.S. I'll have a canary with me . . .

INTERLUDE

Robert Lowell and Elizabeth Bishop see each other in person.
She carries a canary. She puts the canary down.
She shakes Robert Lowell's hand. She is nervous.
It is strangely intimate reading a poem aloud for one other person.
He puts on headphones and records her saying this poem into a microphone:

BISHOP

I caught a tremendous fish
and held him beside the boat
half out of water, with my hook
fast in a corner of his mouth.
He didn't fight.
He hadn't fought at all . . .

I stared and stared
And victory filled up
the little rented boat,
from the pool of bilge
where oil had spread a rainbow
around the rusted engine
to the bailer rusted orange,
the sun-cracked thwarts,
the oarlocks on their strings,
the gunnels—until everything
was rainbow, rainbow, rainbow!

She looks at him.

And I let the fish go.

A moment.
They part.

LOWELL
Dear Elizabeth,

I've at last heard the records and some of them couldn't be better—"Fish" and "Fish-Houses" are wonderful.

Since your visit several weird people have shown up here. Major Dyer, who takes Ezra Pound ice-cream, was a colleague of Patton's and teaches Margaret Truman fencing. And Mrs. Lowell Conger, a mystic and a relative who—but the language fails me, and anyway she's gone back to California.

Affectionately,
Cal

Elizabeth Bishop puts on a sun hat and sunglasses.

BISHOP

Dear Cal,

It has been very pleasant at Hemingway's house but I really couldn't get to work at all of course and am just beginning. The swimming pool is wonderful—it lights up at night—I find that each underwater bulb is five times the voltage of the *one* bulb in the light house across the street, so the pool must be visible to Mars—it is wonderful to swim around in a sort of green fire, one's friends look like luminous frogs.

I received a very obscene letter in verse from Dylan Thomas—*A Streetcar Named Desire* is referred to as "A Truck Called Fuck."

I still think it would be nice if you could visit here sometime, maybe Christmas—if turtle soup can attract you . . .

Affectionately yours,

Elizabeth

LOWELL

Dear Elizabeth,

I tried swimming—was nearly drowned and murdered by children with foot-flippers and helmets and a ferocious mother doing the crawl. Then came down with a cold.

Had a fine week-end with William Carlos Williams. He took me to see his old Spanish mother—91, and was like a Dickens character patting her hands and making her laugh saying, "Mama, would you rather look at us or 20 beautiful blonds?"

I heard Anaïs Nin read—pretty thin stuff, though not unattractive personally.

Key West tempts me.

BISHOP

Happy New Year!

I'm sorry not to have written before. I've been sick most of the last month—asthma—it doesn't completely incapacitate one but is a nuisance. I am feeling much better, maybe the drugs, maybe two new hats, or maybe just getting away from my friends who are so full of solicitude.

LOWELL

So sorry to hear about your asthma—how I thank God that my imaginary asthma was cured by a chiropractor.

Here's my poem, in time I hope to cheer you.

She reads his poem.

BISHOP

I've read your poem. I like it more than I can say. In fact I can shed tears over it very easily & I hardly ever do that except over trash, frequently, & over something at the other extreme, very rarely. I think one weeps over two kinds of embarrassment—& this is so embarrassing in the right way one wants to read it without really looking at it directly. That damned celluloid bird . . .

I made the mistake of reading it when I was working on a poem & it took me an hour or so to get back into my own metre. There are only about 3 words I'd take objection to, at my most carping—

I'm going back to New York in April & hope to stop off in Washington to see a couple of friends—including you—will you be there then?

LOWELL

I'm delighted you liked my poem. I was afraid you'd find it violent and dry.

I won't mail you any more poems, if they take you from writing your own.

How would August be for a visit? Do you think you might have room for my friend Carley? Her little boy is here now, an angelic child, I think, and I'm not soft on children.

BISHOP

I really feel you should *struggle* against your feeling about children, I suppose it's better than drooling over them like Swinburne. But I've always loved the stories about Shelley going around Oxford peering into baby-carriages, and how he once said to a woman carrying a baby, "Madame, can your baby tell us anything of pre-existence?"

LOWELL

My feeling about babies is mostly a joke.

At last my divorce is over. While I was in New York, I saw Jean—all very affectionate and natural, thank God.

It's funny at my age—all the rawness of learning, what I used to think should be done with by twenty-five. Sometimes nothing is so solid to me as writing. I suppose that's what vocation means—at times a torment, a bad conscience, but all in all, purpose and direction, so I'm thankful, and call it good.

BISHOP
Thank you for your letter which did me a great deal of good.

It's very hot today, and I guess I must hike down to that so-called beach and get into that icy water for a while. Having just digested all the *New York Times* and some pretty awful clam-chowder, I don't feel the slightest bit literary, just stupid. Or maybe it's just too much solitude.

Wiscasset is beautiful and dead as a door-nail. I think its heart beats twice a day when the train goes through.

I think almost the last straw here is the hairdresser—a nice big hearty Maine girl. She told me: 1, that my hair "don't feel like hair at all." 2, I was turning gray practically "under her eyes." And when I'd said, yes, I was an orphan, she said "Kind of awful, ain't it, ploughing through life alone." So now I can't walk downstairs in the morning or upstairs at night without feeling I'm ploughing. There's no place like New England.

LOWELL
I know the solitude that gets too much. It doesn't *drug* me, but I get fantastic and uncivilized.

Tell me how to get to your house. Are you sure one more visitor won't be too many? In Maine your friends pour in like lava—hot from their cities. I'll understand if you want a rest.

P.S. There's something haunting and nihilistic about your hair-dresser.

They see each other in Maine.
Suddenly the stage is full of water and a rock.
They stand waist high in cold water, holding hands, looking out.
A silence.
She turns to him.

BISHOP
"When you write my epitaph, you must say I was the loneliest person who ever lived."

She starts laughing at herself.
Suddenly it's not funny.
He stops laughing and touches her face.
A moment.

A SUBTITLE FLASHES:
    He thinks the question: Will you marry me?
    She thinks: What did you say?

The gulls, the sea, and a wave almost engulf them.
They come up for air.
The water dries rapidly.

Part Two: Come to Yaddo

Bishop and Lowell back in their separate spaces, no hint of the sea.

A SUBTITLE FLASHES: August 16, 1947.

BISHOP

Dear Cal,

A commission for you. To find me a rich husband in Washington—one with lots of diamonds and absolutely no interest in the arts.

LOWELL

I'm having a form printed. Age, weight, income, interests, apathies, aversions, and a composite physical examination stamped by a notary.

If you come to Yaddo, you'd find waiting . . . my first project for you: age: 41, weight: 155, hair: full black graying. He has lived for 20 years in a spic and span little white house with two aged servants tending lambs and reading Thoreau.

Outs: He has gone mad once or twice (very stable at present); means small but adequate. I think we'll use him as a decoy.

Here is my starting list: Ted Roethke (only makes $6000 which doesn't cover his drinking, but he has a genius for sponging) . . . My cousins Carlisle and Pearson Winslow, and my Uncle Cot. Really the best of all: 3 houses, a yacht, an income, absolutely no interest in the arts. He's married at the moment to Aunt Sarah but he's already divorced an actress and knows all the ropes.

This is all I've been able to scare up for the first day, but things are in the saddle. You'll make your headquarters here. With each candidate you'll go on a moonlit paddle. We'll see which one you would least know was in the house before five and is most entertaining after five.

Ah me, back to life. I'll write you a serious letter later. You were an angel to put up with all my imbecility and bad behavior. I'm almost a new man thanks to you—or is one ever?

BISHOP

I think you've done an enormous amount of ground-work . . . I must say I like the sound of the uncle best so far—in fact I'd settle for some form of dignified concubinage as long as it was guaranteed . . .

Your room is now occupied by a very cheerful lady-water-colorist who transports a Yogurt-making machine around with her, and also the works of Mary Baker Eddy. I suppose I'm going to find out how she reconciles them, although I don't want to.

I do hope you had a good time in spite of all your troubles, because I did.

They look at each other.

I just hope I didn't get too teasing and opinionated which I guess I'm apt to do with any encouragement at all.

She looks away.

I am alternately thinking of Yaddo & studying my freighter-trip booklets. Can you tell me how one applies to Yaddo?

Affectionately yours,

E.

LOWELL

New thoughts from E's letter: Eliz. equals Betty, you might be called: Eliz, Liz, Lizzie, Betty, Bess, Bessy, Lizbeth or Lisbeth, Ba, Bee, Bet etc. But I guess I'll stick to Elizabeth, though Lizbeth is tempting.

I guess I've emphasized all the charms of Yaddo: large house, trees, space, economy and irresponsibility. Perhaps, you should combine your alternatives—try Yaddo, and if it becomes oppressive, fly away on a freighter.

I *did* enjoy Stonington.

Apologies for this flood of letters . . . Somehow I feel myself again, as I haven't for months, except for bits of Stonington.

During the heat, I've been living on one solid meal, and a detestable thing in blunderbuss glasses, called "orange drink."

I'm feeling fine except:

Thirty-one
Nothing done

keeps going through my head; and I hate to think of packing.

P.S. Next year if our books were done and we had the cash, wouldn't you like to try Italy? The imagination roars with possibilities and inducements.

BISHOP
I sang that song you sing to myself when I was twenty-one, and thirty-one, and I suppose I'll sing it at forty-one. For the meantime I guess my refrain is:

thirty-seven
& far from heaven.

I think you said a while ago that I'd "laugh you to scorn" over some conversation you & I had about how to protect oneself against solitude—but indeed I wouldn't. That's just the kind of "suffering" I'm most at home with & helpless about, I'm afraid, and what with 2 days of fog and alarmingly low tides I've really got it bad & think I'll write you a note before I go out & eat some mackerel.

She looks at a plate of mackerel.
She pushes it aside.
Instead, she takes a sip of red wine.
She puts that aside.
She produces a bottle of whiskey.

If I have any money, & *if* nothing out of the ordinary happens personally, or nothing ordinary, like a war, happens impersonally—I'd like to go to Italy very much. Oh and I think I'll go to Bard for that week-end—will you?

LOWELL
My Bard letter had the phrase: We expect poets like Bishop and what's his name? Yeah, I'm going.

I now have—let me boast—53 stanzas, over 800 lines and am working harder & more steadily than ever in my life. Now shut up about yourself, Cal!

Write some more poems—there are so few in the world now.

A SUBTITLE FLASHES: Bard

INTERLUDE
Bard.
They see each other.
They embrace.
Music.
They toast each other with whiskey.
They dance.
He is suddenly falling-down drunk.
She covers him with a sheet.
He grabs for her hand.
She holds it for a moment.
She takes her hand away.
He grabs it again.

He snores.
She replaces her hand with a wrapped present and flees.

BISHOP
I am so sorry . . .

LOWELL
No! My apologies!

BISHOP
I'll explain it all when I see you—if I can, that is.

LOWELL
This is a before-breakfast letter—I'm sure this practice isn't habit-forming.

BISHOP
I want to hear all that took place after I vanished, and to make my apologies in person—

LOWELL
I've been fingering & weighing and wondering about my present—what happens if you open presents before Christmas?
But I wish you'd come instead.

Bishop sits down with a plate of food and pushes it aside.
She takes a sip of wine.
She pushes it away.
She produces a bottle of whiskey.

An emotional last meeting with Pound: "Cal, god go with you, if you like the company."

Why don't you come for a visit?

Do try to come and spend the night; there's a good morning train—then we can have a fine long evening!

Someone takes away Bishop's wine and whiskey.
She looks at them wistfully.
She then produces a bottle of rubbing alcohol and takes a sip.

But I wish you'd come not for a day, but for the winter. Or summer: I'll settle for that. I'm a bit aghast when I think of how long I'll be on this damned poem. Is anything worth so much work and isolation? Anyhow I wish you weren't so far away.

Elizabeth Bishop throws up.

A final shot. *Look, please, when you are sick tell me, so I won't worry!*

Love & Merry Christmas,
Cal

Bishop dumps the remainder of the rubbing alcohol in the garbage, puts on sunglasses, and moves to Key West.
Sad old-fashioned Christmas music, the kind that plays in a store and makes you want to jump off a bridge.

BISHOP
A postcard:

I have found an absolutely beautiful apartment in Key West—when somebody says "beautiful" about Key West you should really take it with a grain of salt until you've seen it for yourself—in general it is really *awful* & the "beauty" is just the light or something equally perverse.

LOWELL

Now: no number of ingenious postcards is the equivalent of a letter; so really I've written you more than you've me. But I will stock up on what Saratoga has & send them at brief frantic intervals—each one ending "let me hear from you."

Now something I can't tell anyone else. Yesterday Peter Taylor called mostly to warn me that I mustn't pay much attention to his brother-in-law (who is arriving here in ten days). I: "Elizabeth Hardwick is arriving on the same day." Peter: "She's dangerous for you too." I: "Maybe I can interest them in each other." Peter: "Cal, that would be the most blessed thing in the world for you."

Now be a good girl and come to Yaddo.

She looks skeptical about the "good girl" part.

I miss you,
    Cal

BISHOP

I'm afraid I overdid the postcards a little . . .

P.S. I forgot to comment on Elizabeth Hardwick's arrival—*take care.*

LOWELL

This is on your letter and two "Manhattans on rocks" but I do want to write you.

The essential: do come to Yaddo (I'm so lonely) this summer. No, I'm not trying to force your hand.

In a few hours: Miss Hardwick.

BISHOP

All right—I think I shall write to Mrs. Ames right away about Yaddo; tell me what you think would be a good month. July?

LOWELL

Come here in July! There's a little Catholic girl named Flannery O'Connor here now—a real writer, I think. Very moral (in your sense) and witty—whom I'm sure you'd like.

Yaddo has brightened up with Elizabeth Hardwick. Miss Elizabeth is full of talk and high-spirits. For hours last night the nice Yaddonians (Flannery, James, Eliz. and *I*) read Lardner (just sick from laughing) and drank burgundy. A great discovery—you don't get tight or have hangovers and it costs $2.00 a gallon.

I was just making my bed (if you could call it "making") when I became aware of a dull burning smell. "God, I must have left my cigarette burning." I rush into my other room; no cigarette. I feel in my pocket. There, a lighted cigarette in holder consuming a damp piece of Kleenex. The pocket was also stuffed with kitchen matches. Oh my!

The poem is moving again.

I get stuck and in the dumps every so often; but what the hell, that's writing.

Well, lonely girl: good luck & love,

Cal

He begins putting on a tuxedo.

BISHOP

I am mailing you a SAFE if not particularly esthetic ashtray . . .

I was sort of hoping to hear from you . . . I was afraid that, 1. you are sick. 2. you are MAD. 3.—well, various wild fancies.

SUBTITLE: Baldpate Mental Hospital, Georgetown, MA, April 10, 1949, Palm Sunday

LOWELL

I don't know whether you got my last letter or not. I'm in grand shape. The world is full of wonders.

Wedding music.
Robert Lowell stands in a tuxedo.
He waits for an invisible Elizabeth Hardwick to come down the aisle.
During the following, he marches down the aisle beaming.
Rice is thrown at him.
Bishop looks at him getting married.
She is bewildered, then disapproving, then resigned.
And then moved by his happiness.

I wish you great happiness in your marriage and I do hope your troubles are over now for good—you have had too many lately for one person. I've been having quite a few of my own but things seem to have straightened out pretty much now. I was quite at loose ends for this month so finally decided to come here, to Yaddo. There is something a little sinister about the place though, don't you think? I keep getting bats in my room, and then all those awful scummy ponds. But I think what is really the source of the trouble is the *smell*—old lunch boxes I guess . . .

I haven't been able to "work" at all, so spend most of my time very pleasantly sitting on my balcony blowing bubbles.

Give my kindest regards to Elizabeth . . .

She gets out a bubble wand and starts to blow bubbles.
He suddenly lies down, inert.
She suddenly looks concerned, stops blowing bubbles.

Dear Cal:

I was up to New York briefly last week-end and tried to get hold of you but you were out . . . I do hope you're feeling better . . .

With love,
Elizabeth

Things are much better with me. Psycho-therapy is rather amazing—something like stirring up the bottom of an aquarium—chunks of the past coming up at unfamiliar angles, distinct and then indistinct.

We sail now for Europe on the 28th, and plan to go to New York before. Now, I think there's no escaping us for you. *In any case* don't slip away.

She blows bubbles.

Thanks for your goodbye wire. How did you know the ship's address?

She blows bubbles.

A large apartment and maid in Florence all waiting for you. Write me some American gossip, and for heavens' sake hurry over here.

She blows bubbles.

I think I've almost given up expecting you—you'll only come suddenly after swearing you're on your way to Alaska—

She stops blowing bubbles.

I find that every day I less like writing letters and more like getting them; it's the same with poems.

She packs a suitcase.

In May we are going to Rome. Can't you be persuaded to join us? Wine with every meal. Short run-ins with every slight acquaintance of every slight acquaintance you've ever met. But best of all, lots of talk with me. Somehow I haven't made this too attractive.

She snaps her suitcase shut.

Elizabeth and I spent the winter a few feet away from each other, reading. We both enjoy reading aloud to each other and detest listening. Sometimes, I suspect we see too much of one another. Accordingly, I have borrowed a houseboat for four days.

She stands with her suitcase.

Elizabeth has just said the only advantage of marriage is that you can be as gross, slovenly, mean and brutally verbose as you want.

She stands with her suitcase.

You absolutely must leave Yaddo and your horrible archeologist lover and join us in Florence.

She exits.
He looks puzzled, and slightly wounded, watching her exit.

Dear Elizabeth,
   Write soon and tell us about Brazil. Why Brazil?

Brazilian music.

Part Three: Brazil

They age somehow.
Bishop enters.

SUBTITLE: Rio de Janeiro, Brazil, March 21, 1952

BISHOP

Dear Cal,

I wanted to go around the world ending up about now visiting *you*, only they had made some mistake about my reservations on *that* freighter, so I haphazardly settled on South America.

Here I am extremely happy for the first time in my life. I can't quite get used to being "happy," but one remnant of my old morbidity is that I keep fearing that the few people I'm fond of may be in automobile accidents, or suffer some sort of catastrophe . . . The word for even a small accident here is "desastre," so I often have false alarms.

I find the people here frank, startlingly so, and affection-ate, an atmosphere that I just lap up after that dismal winter in Yaddo when I thought my days were numbered. I visited my friend Lota. She wanted me to stay; she offered to build me a studio. I certainly didn't really want to wander around the world in a drunken daze for the rest of my life. So it's all fine & dandy.

For heaven sakes—please keep me informed about your addresses so I can write to you, and I hope you'll write to me. I'm probably going to need it much more than you are.

I have a TOUCAN—named Uncle Sam in a chauvinistic outburst. He's wonderful, gulps down jewelry or pretends to, can play catch with grapes, and has brilliant blue eyes like neon lights.

With love,
Elizabeth

LOWELL

I hear that you are moving to Brazil forever. Hear you're in wonderful tanned, talkative shape with a finished book. I'm talkative but untanned.

Last night I had a dream. I was in France. Paris was again falling to the Germans, but it had become a habit. I went to a party, where I was surrounded by acquaintances. They became distant and shadowy when I approached. Suddenly I saw you and gave you a tremendous hug. You moved to another table. I said: "I know where there are a couple of good French restaurants." You said:

BISHOP

"They're all French here."

LOWELL

You see. You must come back.

BISHOP

I think it was extremely sweet of you to give me a witticism *in a dream*—it shows real, subconscious generosity.

LOWELL

I think about you continually—you and your studio and your Brazilian world. I'm sure you are as happy as you sound. But I don't approve at all. Like a rheumatic old aunt, I would gladly spoil all your fun just to have you back.

You must come and we'll build a replica of your Brazilian house, and you can swing through the years back and forth from one to the other like a pendulum.

BISHOP

We are coming to New York in the spring! Lota is looking forward to breakfast foods. I think we will give a corn-flake party immediately upon arrival . . .

INTERLUDE
Music.
They see each other.
They embrace, friends.
He tries to embrace her more fully.
She looks at him, astonished.
He looks wildly confused.
They go to their separate spaces.
A silence.

Dearest Elizabeth:

I see clearly now that for the last few days I have been living in a state of increasing mania—almost off the rails at the end. It almost seems as if I couldn't be with you any length of time without acting with abysmal myopia and lack of consideration. My disease gives one (during its seizures) a headless heart.

Also I want you to know that you need never again fear my overstepping myself and stirring up confusion with you. There's one bit of the past that I would like to get off my chest and then I think all will be easy with us.

The lights become lights of a swimming and sunning day.
The stage fills with water and a rock.
He goes to her and speaks this letter directly to her.
They sit on a rock, or the idea of a rock.

Do you remember how at the end of that long swimming and sunning day we went up to, I think, the relatively re-moved upper Gross house and had one of those real fried New England dinners, probably awful. And we were talking about this and that about ourselves and you said rather humorously yet it was truly meant,

BISHOP
"When you write my epitaph, you must say I was the loneliest person who ever lived."

Probably you forget, and anyway all that is mercifully changed since you found Lota. But at the time, I guess (I don't want to overdramatize) our relations seemed to have reached a new place. I assumed it would be just a matter of time before I proposed and I half believed that you would accept. Yet I wanted it all to have the right build-up. Well, I didn't say anything then. And of course it wasn't the right stage-setting, and then there was that poetry conference at Bard and I remember one evening presided over by Mary McCarthy and my Elizabeth was there, and going home to the Bard poets' dormitory, I was so drunk that my hands turned cold and I felt half-dying and held your hand.

And nothing was said, and like a loon that needs sixty feet, I believe, to take off from the water, I wanted time and space, and went on assuming, and when I was to have joined you at Key West I was determined to ask you. Really for so callous (I fear) a man, I was fearfully shy and scared of spoiling things and distrustful of being steady enough to be the least good. Then of course the Yaddo explosion came and all was over.

The water recedes.

Yet there were a few months. And of course our friendship really wasn't a courting, was really disinterested (bad phrase) really led to no encroachments. So it is.

Let me say this though and then leave the matter forever; I do think free will is sewn into everything we do; you can't cross a street, light a cigarette, drop saccharine in your coffee without really doing it. Yet the possible alternatives that life allows us are very few, often there must be none. I've never thought there was any choice for me about writing poetry. No doubt if I used my head better, ordered my life better, worked harder, the poetry would be improved, and there must be many lost poems, innumerable accidents and ill-done actions.

But asking you is *the* might have been for me, the one towering change, the other life that might have been had.

It was that way for these nine years or so that intervened. It was deeply buried, and this spring and summer it boiled to the surface. Now it won't happen again. It won't happen, I'm really underneath utterly *in* love and sold on my Elizabeth, and it's a great solace to me that you are with Lota, and I am sure it is the will of the heavens that all is as it is.

He hands her a record.

P.S. The last part is too heatedly written with too many *ands* and so forth. The record is French Renaissance Vocal Music.

She takes the record. She closes her eyes.
Music.
She opens her eyes.

Love,
    Cal

She looks out, not knowing what to say.
Blackout.
Intermission.

ACT TWO

Part One: Skunk

LOWELL
P.S. The last part is too heatedly written with too many *ands* and so forth. The record is French Renaissance Vocal Music.

She takes the record.

Love,
  Cal

She puts the record on.
She picks up a pen.
She tries to write.
She stops and crumples the paper.
She tries again.

SUBTITLE: 115 East 67th Street, New York, August 28, 1957

BISHOP
Dearest Cal:

I wanted to answer your wonderful letter right away . . .
but . . .

She stops.
Meanwhile he climbs a ladder.

But we've been so busy . . . And I'm apt to be interrupted
at any moment by my Brazilian friends returning from
Bloomingdale's.

LOWELL
Asking you is *the* might have been—

BISHOP
I don't know how Lota does it, really; I hate to shop so.

A moon appears.

LOWELL
—the other life that might have been had—

He reaches the top of the ladder and tries to grab the moon.
The moon won't budge.

BISHOP
New York is awful I think.

LOWELL
I am sure it is the will of the heavens—

BISHOP

After racking my brains I just this minute decided it is like a battered-up old alarm clock that insists on gaining five or six hours a day & has to be kept lying on its side.

LOWELL

So it is . . .

BISHOP

I do hope you're feeling much, much better, Cal, and realize now that I may not have written a very cheering letter.

She is not cheerful.

With lots of love as always—
    Elizabeth

She puts her head in her hands.
He jumps off the ladder.
Or appears to jump off a ladder.
But maybe he just disappears into thin air.

The record ends.
He reappears.
She looks up.

LOWELL

I want you and Lota to know that I *am* at last in reverse. I am taking my anti-manic pills—75 mgs. of sparine, no more than what my doctor prescribed on the bottle but too much to drive or even see people much. The effect is something like the slowing and ache of a medium fever.

I want you to know . . . Oh, dear, I wanted you to know so many things . . .

Yesterday was mostly bed and letting my beard grow. Today I feel certain that I am not going off the deep end.

One is left strangely dumb, and talking about the past is like a cat's trying to explain climbing down a ladder. Gracelessly, like a standing child trying to sit down, like a cat or a coon coming down a tree, I'm getting down my ladder to the moon. Ask Lota to forgive me. And forgive me yourself, dear old friend. I'll make no solo descents on you either in New York or Brazil.

He walks to her and gives her a book.
A rare volume of George Herbert that was in his family for many years.

P.S. The George Herbert! I've really always wanted you to have it. I'll be mortally hurt if you don't keep it.

BISHOP
Thank you for the book. This is the first time I'd ever gone traveling without George Herbert so it is nice to have him again—even if I feel you really really shouldn't have given it away. I've been reading him a lot—

LOWELL
Thy mouth was open, but thou couldst not sing—

BISHOP

I think we should read his "Treatise of Temperance & Sobriety" out loud to each other. It begins "Having observed in my time many of my friends, of excellent wit & noble disposition, overthrown & undone by Intemperance; who, if they had lived, could have been an ornament to the world and a comfort to their friends . . ."

Dear Cal, do please please take care of yourself and be an ornament to the world (you're already that) and a comfort to your friends . . . There *are* many hopeful things, too, you know. Sobriety & gayety & patience & toughness will do the trick. Or so I hope for myself & pray for you too.

You weren't "inconsiderate," Cal! You were a wonderful host, and we had such a nice time with you, really. Even if Lota does think all fir trees are deliberately planted, she liked Maine very much.

I'll write soon—

LOWELL

Dearest Elizabeth,

We are going to have a child.

She looks surprised.
Then melancholy.
Her greatest regret in the world is not having a child.

LOWELL

It will come sometime in January, and already *we* are exhausted. We lie about on sofas all day eating cornflakes, no-calorie ginger-ale and yogurt. Elizabeth never moves except to turn the page of an English newspaper or buy a dress. I never move except to turn on my high-fi radio or to go on expeditions for second-hand books . . . We hear of women who ski all through pregnancy, give birth in bomb shelters, but we don't approve, and are timid, delicate, and ante-bellum. We are so much older than other beginning parents.

How we boast! People whom I had utterly felt cut off from: my barber, my dentist, the head of the Boston University English department, wives of friends, children . . . to all of them I can't stop talking and bragging.

Elizabeth Bishop feeds her toucan.

LOWELL
Do you stop in the States on your way to Europe? I wish with all my heart that you could somehow stretch things and see us. We seem attached to each other by some stiff piece of wire, so that each time one moves, the other moves in another direction. We should call a halt to that.

A horizontal wire comes down from the ceiling, connecting them.
It is something of a pulley, or an old-fashioned thing children used to make to connect one attic with another, and attach items in between, or pretend to use the telephone on either end.
A baby cries.
Bishop hears. She smiles.
She attaches a postcard to the stiff piece of wire.
It travels across the stage to him.

LOWELL

Our little girl, Harriet Winslow Lowell was just born last Friday, weight 6 pounds and 14 ounces, and already more with both feet on the ground than her fatuous and boasting parents.

He receives her postcard.

BISHOP

Just a note of congratulation on the arrival of Harriet Winslow Lowell. What should I bring her from Brazil, I wonder? Lota is magnificent with child-problems. I suspect it's because she's had so much practice with me.

LOWELL

Upstairs, Harriet Winslow Lowell is crying as rhythmically as breathing. Lizzie and our beaverlike professional baby nurse, Miss Elsemore, are not in theoretic or emotional agreement. Poor Lizzie isn't allowed to play with Harriet except for thirty minutes between six and six-thirty when she would like to be relaxing over an Old Fashioned.

I'm really mad about my little daughter and feel as though I had been up to now lacking some prime faculty: eyesight, hearing, reason.

BISHOP

Miss Elsemore sounds terrifying. It's funny how caring for helpless babies builds character.

You probably know all about the Pulitzer business . . . I was really surprised . . . It was very funny here—a reporter from *O Globo* shouting at me over the telephone, and I kept replying in a cool New Englandy way, "Thank you very much," and he shouted again, "But dona Elizabetchy, don't you understand? O Prémio Pulitzer!"

Well, one never knows about these things, or how one *should* feel about them. I am taking the money, or part of it, to buy a high-fidelity victrola.

LOWELL

I am so delighted by the Pulitzer. I was on the National Book Award committee and tried to get the prize given to you and/or Randall. Your chances were killed by Phyllis McGinley who thought you were serious or a woman or something.

I've read your poems many times. I think I read you with more interest than anyone now writing. I know I do, but I think I would even if it weren't for personal reasons. I feel that I write only for you and Lizzie. I'm dedicating "Skunk Hour" to you. A skunk isn't much of a present for a Lady Poet, but I'm a skunk in the poem.

She reads his poem aloud.

BISHOP

One dark night,
my Tudor Ford climbed the hill's skull;
I watched for love-cars. Lights turned down,
they lay together, hull to hull,
where the graveyard shelves on the town. . . .
My mind's not right.

LOWELL

A car radio bleats,
"Love, O careless Love. . . ." I hear
my ill-spirit sob in each blood cell,
as if my hand were at its throat. . . .
I myself am hell;

BISHOP

nobody's here—

She puts down the poem.

LOWELL

We've talked over a lot of things together I've never mentioned to Elizabeth. If you ever feel like writing me privately
(I don't mean anything by this)—

She looks suspicious.

BISHOP

I don't know why I haven't been able to write to you sooner,
really.

LOWELL

—you can address the letter c/o The Dept. of English,
Boston University.

BISHOP

I don't often get these letter-writing blocks, & particularly
about my favorite correspondents.

I really glory in the memory of your visit and miss you terribly.

All the way down on our freighter I composed endless letters to you, full of profound new ideas, but they just evaporated into the ocean air.

So glad you liked the Purcell. I had intended to send you, for Christmas, "Dido & Aeneas," but I wasn't sure whether you had it or not.

Music plays, Purcell.

My idea is to wean you away from those French songs, because I think the English ones are so much better and so much more appropriate to us!

I'd be particularly charmed to have "Skunk Hour" dedicated to me. I started a poem to you and Marianne Moore two years ago, called "Letter to Two Friends." It is rather light, though. Oh heavens, when does one begin to write the *real* poems? I certainly feel as if I never had. But of course I don't feel that way about yours. They all seem real as real— and getting more so— They all have that sure feeling, as if you'd been in a stretch when everything and anything suddenly seemed material for poetry—or not material, seemed to *be* poetry. If only one could see everything that way all the time. It seems to me it's the whole purpose of art—that rare feeling of control, illuminating—life *is* all right, for the time being.

And here I must confess that I am green with envy of your kind of assurance.

He lies down.

In some ways you are the luckiest poet I know!—in some ways not so lucky, either, of course. But it is hell to realize one has wasted half one's talent through timidity that probably could have been overcome if anyone in one's family had had a few grains of sense or education . . . Well, maybe it's not too late!

He rubs his temples.

January 29th, I think—1958, I know

I began to worry a bit when I didn't receive any answer to my two long letters to you before Christmas, then I heard that you'd been sick, so I wrote Elizabeth. I do hope and pray you are feeling yourself again. (Not that I pray very much, but I mean the intensity of hoping . . .)

Robert Lowell gets up.

LOWELL
Almost immediately after writing you my last letter, I wanted to write another taking it back. Elizabeth and I are happily back together . . . after the voyage to Somes Sound. It was rich in undramatic mishaps. We went ashore . . . Elizabeth had drunk a whole water tumbler of the martinis to which she is allergic. She sprawled on the fore-cabin and began to

discuss sotto voce an amazingly frank and detailed reappraisal of our entire marriage. It went on for an hour and a half. She said that we were all leaving the next day for Boston where we would both go to doctors.

Now I spend long week-ends at home and will soon leave the hospital entirely. I am part of my family again, I love my family again.

I live in an interesting house at McLean's Hospital, one which no man had entered since 1860; suddenly it was made co-ed. It was like entering some ancient deceased sultan's seraglio. The man next to me is a Harvard Law professor. One day, he is all happiness, giving the plots of Trollope novels, and on another day, I hear cooing pigeon sounds, and if I listen carefully, the words: "Oh terror, TERROR!"

BISHOP

McLean's is a good place, I think. My mother stayed there once for a long time. However, I hope you don't have to stay very long—the people are so fascinating I think one begins to find the usual world a bit dull by comparison.

My darling toucan died. It was all my fault. I used an insecticide the man in the store said was "inoffensive" to animals, and it killed him. There he lay, just like life only with his feet up in the air. I want to get another one, but Lota says we're having a little vacation from toucans now.

I seem to be writing poems again at last—they are all such old poems, though, it's like cleaning up the attic. Wishing I could start writing poetry all over again on another planet.

A planet comes down. She approaches it.

LOWELL

Such an age since I've heard from you. Your telegram was a
joy, but I was grieved to think of the lost letter. Please write
it again . . .

She gets on her planet.

BISHOP (*composing on her planet*)
Let Shakespeare & Milton
Stay at a Hilton—
I shall stay
At Chico Rei—

She shakes her head and tries again.

Marianne, loan me a noun!
Cal, please cable a verb!
Or simply propulse through the ether
some more powerful meter . . .

LOWELL
For Elizabeth Bishop 4:
Have you seen an inchworm crawl on a leaf,
cling to the very end, revolve in air,
feeling for something to reach to something? Do
you still hang your words in air, ten years
unfinished, glued to your notice board, with gaps
or empties for the unimaginable phrase—
unerring Muse who makes the casual perfect?

He looks up from his book. They look at each other.
He yells up to her on her planet.

On, Dear, with those painful, very large unfinished poems!

She writes a poem, "The Armadillo," which she dedicates to
Lowell.

BISHOP
For Robert Lowell:

This is the time of year
when almost every night
the frail, illegal fire balloons appear.
Climbing the mountain height,

rising toward a saint
still honored in these parts,
the paper chambers flush and fill with light
that comes and goes, like hearts.

Once up against the sky it's hard
to tell them from the stars—
planets, that is—the tinted ones:
Venus going down, or Mars . . .

She gets off her planet.

I hope you aren't thinking that I am *a*: dead *b*: annoyed. I'm
neither; but I did have *flu*.

LOWELL

I am back from a month in the sanitarium . . .

BISHOP

I made up my mind to go to teach in the States. I don't want
to one bit, but need the money.

Lota hates having me go—very nice of her—but after a
sad scene she is now resigned!

LOWELL

The day after tomorrow, I'll be fifty, and Lizzie is arranging
a party of almost thirty . . .

BISHOP

Well, now I know when your birthday is— Many happy re-
turns. I minded being 35 very much, but haven't been able to
give a damn since—there are too many other things that one
can do a *little* something about, possibly.

LOWELL

I seem to spend my life missing you!

BISHOP

Well, now I'm in New York. The plan is that as soon as Lota
is well enough she will join me . . .

I went out this afternoon and again spotted you looking
very unhappy, this time on the *New York Review of Books* . . .
It is nice to be on the same continent with you again!

Found a lovely word—you probably know it—ALLELO-
MIMETIC. (Don't DARE use it!)

SUBTITLE: Lota commits suicide.

Elizabeth Bishop looks up.
She falls over.
Lowell picks her up and steadies her.

LOWELL
It was a joy being with you, even in this sad time—all the more perhaps because the sorrow can be shared a little.

I feel for Lota, though I've no right to; a part of my life has fallen away, a part of my life in you.

I enclose a poem to you, the old Castine poem I could never finish. You may not like it, or what it says, but I hope you will.

The stage becomes the memory of sea and rock again, with no real water.

It was a Maine fishing town—
. . . Remember?

BISHOP
We sat on a slab of rock.

LOWELL
From this distance in time
it seems the color
of iris, rotting and turning purpler,

BISHOP
but it was only
the usual gray rock

turning the usual green
when drenched by the sea.

LOWELL
The sea drenched the rock
at our feet all day . . .

BISHOP
We wished our two souls
might return like gulls
to the rock.

LOWELL
In the end,
the water was too cold for us.

The sea recedes.

BISHOP
Oh, thank you; thank you very much—you can really never
know how much this has cheered me up and made me feel a
bit like myself again.

I love my poem—and you, too, of course . . .

I have two minor questions, but, as usual, they have to
do with my George-Washington-handicap. I can't tell a lie
even for art, apparently; it takes an awful effort or a sudden
jolt to make me alter facts. Shouldn't it be a *lobster* town,
rather than fishing town . . .

He smiles. And revises, with a pencil.

My passion for accuracy may strike you as old-maidish—
but since we do float on an unknown sea I think we should
examine the other floating things that come our way very
carefully; who knows what might depend on it?

LOWELL
I worry about you so and wish you'd come home.

BISHOP
Well, you are right to worry about me, only please DON'T!—
I am pretty worried about myself. I am trying to sell the
house, go through all the books, papers, letters—about 3,000
or more books here . . . meanwhile it is too damned lonely
and disagreeable and I have not been able to work. There are
endless interruptions, noise, confusion, thefts. I really love my
house and would like to stay in it, if—if—if things were dif-
ferent. The very thought of all the packing makes me sick—
and then, where to go? How to live? I miss Lota more every
day of my life.

The stage darkens.
He sends her a lantern on a pulley.

Have you ever gone through caves?—I did once, in Mexico,
and hated it . . . Finally, after hours of stumbling along, one
sees daylight ahead—a faint blue glimmer—and it never looked
so wonderful before. That's what I feel as though I were
waiting for now—just the faintest glimmer that I'm going to
get out of this somehow, alive. Meanwhile—your letter has
helped tremendously—like being handed a lantern.

She takes the lantern.

Now I must pack an overnight bag and try to lock up this too unlockable house and try not to think of what will be missing when I get back—it gets to be a sort of game: what goes next? Or, how many things can you count that are missing in this room? How many beginning with A? With B?

She looks for something underneath a pile of papers.
She throws the papers on the floor.
She looks wildly for something.
She finds it.
It is a poem that she wrote, "One Art."

The art of losing isn't hard to master;
so many things seem filled with the intent
to be lost that their loss is no disaster.

Lose something every day. Accept the fluster
of lost door keys, the hour badly spent.
The art of losing isn't hard to master.

Then practice losing farther, losing faster:
places, and names, and where it was you meant
to travel. None of these will bring disaster.

I lost my mother's watch. And look! my last, or
next-to-last, of three loved houses went.
The art of losing isn't hard to master.

I lost two cities, lovely ones. And, vaster,
some realms I owned, two rivers, a continent.
I miss them, but it wasn't a disaster.

—Even losing you (the joking voice, a gesture
I love) I shan't have lied. It's evident
the art of losing's not too hard to master
though it may look like

LOWELL
(*Write* it!)

BISHOP
like disaster.

Part Two: Art just isn't worth that much

They age somehow.

SUBTITLE: 1970

LOWELL

Dearest Elizabeth,

Lizzie and I have more or less separated, though as good-naturedly as such things can be. I have someone else. And the future looks cheerful, but who at our age can ever tell?

My "someone" is Caroline Citkowitz. She is 39, has published stories in the London Magazine, has three very pretty daughters, and was once married to Freud's grandson, Lucian. What a bare list, but how can I make the introduction? She is very beautiful and saw me through my sickness with wonderful kindness. I suppose I shouldn't forget Harriet and Lizzie, anyway I can't.

BISHOP

I am glad the lady is beautiful; that really cheers one a lot.

LOWELL

The child will be born in October. We have three little girls, and this strangely makes the arrival of another much less disturbing . . .

BISHOP

I think it is nice that it is a little boy—the possibilities were limited, of course, but a change is interesting . . .

He walks over and hands her a manuscript.

LOWELL

Read *Dolphin* when you have leisure. I am going to publish, and don't want advice, except for yours. Lizzie won't like it.

Bishop reads The Dolphin.
She looks disapproving.
She puts the book down, hard.

BISHOP

I've re-read *The Dolphin* a good many times now . . . Please believe that I think it is wonderful poetry. It is also honest poetry—*almost*. I have one tremendous and awful BUT.

　　If you were any other poet I can think of I certainly wouldn't attempt to say anything at all; I wouldn't think it was worth it. But because it is you, and a great poem (I've never used the word "great" before), and I love you a lot—I feel I must tell you what I really think.

　　Don't be alarmed. Here is a quotation from dear little Hardy: "What should certainly be protested against, in cases where there is no authorization, is the mixing of fact and fiction in unknown proportions. Infinite mischief would lie in that."

I'm sure my point is only too plain . . . Lizzie is not dead—but there is a "mixture of fact & fiction," and you have *changed* her letters. That is "infinite mischief," I think. One can use one's life as material—one does, anyway—but these letters—aren't you violating a trust? IF you were given permission—IF you hadn't changed them . . . But *art just isn't worth that much.* I keep remembering Hopkins' marvelous letter about the idea of a "gentleman" being the highest thing ever conceived—higher than a "Christian" even, certainly than a poet. It is not being "gentle" to use personal letters that way—it's cruel.

In general, I deplore the "confessional"—however, when you wrote LIFE STUDIES perhaps it was a necessary movement, and it helped make poetry more real, fresh and immediate. But now—ye gods—anything goes, and I am so sick of poems about the students' mothers & fathers and sex-lives and so on.

I can't bear to have anything you write tell what we're really like in 1972 . . . perhaps it's as simple as that. DOLPHIN is marvelous—no doubt about that—I'll write you all the things I like sometime!

LOWELL

Let me write you right away . . . my first scattered impressions—my thanks. Most of your reservations seem likely to be right and useful. I am talking about your brief line to line objections—

BISHOP

I was so relieved to get your letter—I was awfully afraid I'd been crude, rude . . . However, I think you've misunderstood me a little.

LOWELL

I did not see Lizzie's letters as slander, but as sympathetic, though necessarily awful for her to read. I took out the worst things written against me, so as not to seem self-pitying. I could say the letters are cut, doctored, part fiction . . .

BISHOP

My point was that one *can't* mix fact & fiction— What I have objected to in your use of the letters is that I think you've changed them—& you had no right to do that. I do see how when you have written an absolutely wonderful, or satisfactory, poem—it's hard to think of changing anything . . .

LOWELL

It's oddly enough a technical problem as well as a gentleman's problem. How can the story be told at all without the letters? It's the revelation of a wife wanting her husband not to leave her, and who does leave her. That's the trouble, not the mixture of truth and fiction. No one would object if I said Lizzie was wearing a purple and red dress, when it was yellow.

BISHOP

I feel I've annoyed you more than enough, but I can't resist this from Kierkegaard:

LOWELL

The trouble is the letters make the book; they make Lizzie
real beyond my invention . . .

BISHOP

"The law of delicacy, according to which an author has a
right to use what he himself has experienced—

She has an asthma attack.

BISHOP   LOWELL
is that he is never to utter   How can I want to hurt?
  verity   Hurt Lizzie and Harriet?
but is to keep verity
for himself & only let it be
  refracted—"

LOWELL

How can the story be told without the letters?

BISHOP

I don't give a damn what someone like Mailer writes about
his wives—but I DO give a damn what you write!

A silence.
She tries to catch her breath, wheezing.
He calls her on the telephone.
She wheezes, trying to speak, and can't.

BISHOP

You talk—I can't—

They hang up.
A silence.

LOWELL

I'm afraid the unexpected sadness of speaking to you, made me speechless. When you said "You talk, I can't," I could only think of questions and became speechless. But we are never speechless together.

I must write more softly to you. Forgive me.

They age somehow.

BISHOP

I am NOT going to hear Stanley Kunitz in Madison Square. What are we coming to? You can't read poems without a drum & guitar and a bit of chanting . . .

Why all this change? My favorite eye shadow—for years—suddenly comes in 3 cakes in a row and one has to use all one's skill to avoid *iridescence* . . .

LOWELL

I see us still when we first met, at Randall's. I see you as rather tall, long brown-haired, shy but full of description and anecdote as now. I was brown haired and thirty I guess. I was largely invisible to myself, and nothing I knew how to look at. But the fact is we were swimming in our young age, with the water coming down on us, and we were gulping.

BISHOP

Cal dear, maybe your memory *is* failing!— Never, never was I "tall"— And I never had "long brown hair" either!—

It started turning gray when I was 23—and probably was already somewhat grizzled when I first met you. I think you must be seeing someone else! What I remember about that meeting is your dishevelment, your lovely curly hair, and how we talked about a Picasso show—and how much I liked you, after having been almost too scared to go. You were also rather dirty, which I rather liked, too.

Well I must stop and slice some green beans— See you later, alligator, as they say in Florida.

So *please* don't put me in a beautiful poem tall with long brown hair!

She sits and looks out a window.
She grips the chair as though it is a wheelchair.

LOWELL

Frank told me you arrived back in Boston in a wheelchair, a sad surprise because you seemed in such good health here and safe with your new English drug. Hope you are now recovered and moving to North Haven. I think on clear days you can see Castine from the northern shore. I miss it all.

My book is done. It's the opposite of yours, bulky, rearranged, added-to—as though the unsatiated appetite were demanding a solid extra course when dinner was meant to be over. I spent a week or more on three lines which finally ended in changing the position of two words. I think a lot about getting things right—and often there is sprawl that cannot be arranged. We seem to be near our finish, so near the final, the perfect, is forbidden us, not even in the game.

I have no more to say . . . of course.

He hails a taxi.

BISHOP
I'm writing to you this morning to say that I hope you'll understand if I say I'd rather you *don't* come to North Haven on the 10th . . .

He looks over as though he sees her.
Just for a moment, while crossing the street.
Then Robert Lowell has a heart attack and lies down.

Day before yesterday and the day before that, seven, in all, guests left & although I love them all and we'd had a very nice time—it was just a bit too much. I hope you'll understand when I say I *must* work and not break off for a while.

He closes his eyes.

SUBTITLE: Robert Lowell has a heart attack in a taxi.

He dies.

BISHOP
I've been reading your DOMESDAY BOOK—it's just about perfect, I think—I'd only question "splash flowers" . . . (Forgive my being so picky.) There are many, many good— no, gorgeous lines—I'll show you my underlinings sometime—

Well, I'll see you in Cambridge or New York—and maybe in North Haven next summer—

She looks up sharply.
She breathes in.
Then she stands up and reads the following poem.
While she reads, Robert Lowell casually rises from the dead.
He leans against a wall and listens to the poem.

BISHOP
North Haven
In memoriam: Robert Lowell

The goldfinches are back, or others like them,
and the white-throated sparrow's five-note song,
pleading and pleading, brings tears to the eyes.
Nature repeats herself, or almost does:
repeat, repeat, repeat; revise, revise, revise.

Years ago, you told me it was here
(in 1932?) you first "discovered girls"
and learned to sail, and learned to kiss.
You had "such fun," you said, that classic summer.
("Fun"—it always seemed to leave you at a loss . . .)

He smiles.

You left North Haven, anchored in its rock,
afloat in mystic blue . . . And now—you've left
for good. You can't derange, or rearrange,
your poems again. (But the sparrows can their song.)
The words won't change again. Sad friend, you cannot
change.

Lowell quietly applauds.
She turns to him.
She walks toward him.
During the following exchange, thousands of letters pour down on them,
slowly, as they took some time getting over various oceans.

They un-age somehow.

LOWELL
Dear Miss Bishop

BISHOP
Dear Mr. Lowell

LOWELL
Dear Elizabeth

BISHOP
Dear Cal

LOWELL
Dearest Elizabeth

BISHOP
Dearest Cal

LOWELL
Affectionately, Cal

BISHOP
Recessively yours, Elizabeth

LOWELL

My darling receding Elizabeth . . .

They reach each other.

BISHOP

I don't know why I've been so slow about writing to you,
since I think of you every day of my life I'm sure—

LOWELL

Dearest friend, I miss you so—

He takes her hands.

BISHOP

I'll write soon—

He shakes his head, as in: You can't write to dead people.
She nods, as in: I will write to you.
They look at the letters.

And it is as though they have become their own words.
And so can remain in the same place.
They exit, together.
The end.

Afterword

Anyone doing a complete production of the play should also have *Words in Air: The Complete Correspondence Between Elizabeth Bishop and Robert Lowell*. The letters from the play correspond to the following letters, which are numbered and dated in that book as follows. Occasionally, text from two or three letters has been combined, in which case the number and date refer to the letter or letters from which the text was primarily drawn. The letters are not always quoted verbatim.

  9 1. 46 King Street, New York, May 12th, 1947
 9–10 2. 202 E. 15th St., New York, New York, May 23, 1947
 10–11 3. Briton Cove, Cape Breton, August 14th, 1947
  11 4. Yaddo, Saratoga Springs, August 21, 1947
  12 6. New York, N.Y., September 22nd, 1947
  13 12. November 3, 1947
  14 13. Key West, Florida, November 18th, 1947
 14–15 14. November 20, 1947
  15 18. 630 Dey Street, Key West, Florida, January 1st, 1948
  15 19. January 21, 1948
 15–16 23. March 18th, 1948
  16 24. Washington, D.C., March 22, 1948
  16 33. Wiscasset, Maine, June 30th, 1948
 16–17 34. July 2, 1948
  17 35. Sunday, July 11th, 1948
 17–18 36. July 14, 1948
 19–20 43. Ipswich, Massachusetts, August 16, 1948

64–65 442. January 16th, 1975
  66 459. August 2nd, 1977

The play mostly follows the chronology of the letters with some exceptions. I've suggested some subtitles for dates that signify leaps in time or jumps in location. But I think to make the reader, or audience, overly aware of dates and place would be to make the play overly biographical. The play should have, instead, the flavor of an intimate conversation that manages to be intimate because matters like time and place are increasingly irrelevant.

Also, the letter that begins "Dear Cal, A commission for you" is taken from a letter Elizabeth Bishop wrote to Carley Dawson about Robert Lowell in *One Art*, p. 165. The fragment beginning "Marianne, loan me a noun/Cal, please cable a verb!" is from "Letter to Two Friends," in *Edgar Allan Poe & The Juke-Box: Uncollected Poems, Drafts, and Fragments* by Elizabeth Bishop, p. 113. The fragment beginning "Let Shakespeare and Milton" is from "Let Shakespeare and Milton," in *Edgar Allan Poe & The Juke-Box*, p. 126.

Acknowledgments

I am grateful to James Bundy and Jennifer Kiger at Yale Repertory Theatre for commissioning the play and seeing it through. Many thanks to Les Waters for signing on to direct the play when it was only a series of fragments. To Tony Taccone at Berkeley Repertory Theatre for understanding that playwrights need two productions to finish plays. To Mary Beth Fisher, Jefferson Mays, and Tom Nelis—your incarnations will live with me always. To Vassar Library. To Brian Kulick. To Zak Berkman, and the amazing Ellen Mclaughlin and Ronda Eckert. To Polly Noonan and the Poetry Foundation in Chicago. To André Bishop for hosting the first reading of the play and Cynthia Nixon for reading. To Harriet Lowell for trusting me. Thanks to Jonathan Galassi for having faith in the project. To Mitzi Angel. To Kay Jamison. To Tom Paulin. To Thomas Travisano and Saskia Hamilton for their beautiful scholarship. I recommend *Becoming a Poet: Elizabeth Bishop with Marianne Moore and Robert Lowell* by David Kalstone, *Remembering Elizabeth Bishop: An Oral Biography* by Gary Fountain and Peter Brazeau, and *One Art: Letters* selected and edited by Robert Giroux. Many thanks to early readers Andy Bragen, Tony Charuvastra, Maria Dizzia, Rinne Groff, Todd London, and Kathleen Ruhl. Thank you to dear Kathleen Tolan for telling me to read *Words in Air*, and for being a beacon of literary friendship over the years. The same holds true for Andy Bragen, who tirelessly supported this play in its embryonic stages. My biggest debt is owed to Robert Lowell and Elizabeth Bishop, two of the most beautiful letter writers in the history of letters.